Biodiversity

of Woodlands

GREG PYERS

Marshall Cavendish
Benchmark
New York

This edition first published in 2011 in the United States of America by
MARSHALL CAVENDISH BENCHMARK
An imprint of Marshall Cavendish Corporation

Website: www.marshallcavendish.us

This publication represents the opinions and views of the author based on Greg Pyer's personal experience, knowledge, and research. The information in this book serves as a general guide only. The author and publisher have used their best efforts in preparing this book and disclaim liability rising directly and indirectly from the use and application of this book.

Other Marshall Cavendish Offices:
Marshall Cavendish Ltd. 5th Floor, 32-38 Saffron Hill, London EC1N 8 FH, UK • Marshall Cavendish International (Asia) Private Limited, 1 New Industrial Road, Singapore 536196 • Marshall Cavendish International (Thailand) Co Ltd. 253 Asoke, 12th Flr, Sukhumvit 21 Road, Klongtoey Nua, Wattana, Bangkok 10110, Thailand • Marshall Cavendish (Malaysia) Sdn Bhd, Times Subang, Lot 46, Subang Hi-Tech Industrial Park, Batu Tiga, 40000 Shah Alam, Selangor Darul Ehsan, Malaysia

Marshall Cavendish is a trademark of Times Publishing Limited

All websites were available and accurate when this book was sent to press.

Library of Congress Cataloging-in-Publication Data

Pyers, Greg.
   Biodiversity of woodlands / Greg Pyers.
      p. cm. — (Biodiversity)
   Includes index.
   Summary: "Discusses the variety of living things in a woodland ecosystem"—Provided by publisher.
   ISBN 978-1-60870-074-5
   1. Forest biodiversity—Juvenile literature. 2. Forest ecology—Juvenile literature.
   3. Endangered ecosystems—Juvenile literature. I. Title.
   QH86.P944 2010
577.3—dc22

                                                                              2009042315

First published in 2010 by
MACMILLAN EDUCATION AUSTRALIA PTY LTD
15–19 Claremont Street, South Yarra 3141

Visit our website at www.macmillan.com.au or go directly to www.macmillanlibrary.com.au

Associated companies and representatives throughout the world.

Copyright © Greg Pyers 2010

Edited by Georgina Garner
Text and cover design by Kerri Wilson
Page layout by Kerri Wilson
Photo research by Legend Images
Illustrations by Richard Morden

Printed in China

Acknowledgments
The author and the publisher are grateful to the following for permission to reproduce copyright material:

Front cover photograph of the Serengeti landscape, Kenya, © Fernando Rodrigues/Shutterstock.
Back cover photograph of a rhinocerous © Artur Tiutenko/Shutterstock.

Photographs courtesy of:
© Cliff & Dawn Frith/ANTPhoto.com, **13**; © Denis O'Byrne/ANTPhoto.com, **19**; © Patricio Robles Gil/AUSCAPE, **15**; © Raymond Gehman/Corbis, **29**; Tim Laman/Getty Images, **27**; © 2008 Jupiterimages Corporation, **10**; Photodisc/Robert Glusic, **18**; Photolibrary/ DV, **22**; Photolibrary/David Hay Jones, **24**; Photolibrary/Gregory MD., **23**; Photolibrary/Nigel Pavitt, **9** (bottom); Photolibrary/Carl R. Sams II, **4**; Picture Media/REUTERS/Romeo Ranoco, **21**; Picture Media/REUTERS/Rick Wilking, **20**; © dirkr/Shutterstock, **25**; © David Hyde/Shutterstock, **17**; © Jim Parkin/Shutterstock, **16**; © Fernando Rodrigues/Shutterstock, **1**, **11**;© Leonid Smirnov/ Shutterstock, **7**; Wikimedia Commons, **28**; The Wilderness Society, photo by Barbara Madden, **9** (top).

Quote by Charles Nordhoff from http://laspilitas.com/nature-of-california/communities/central-oak-woodland, **29**.

While every care has been taken to trace and acknowledge copyright, the publisher tenders their apologies for any accidental infringement where copyright has proved untraceable. Where the attempt has been unsuccessful, the publisher welcomes information that would redress the situation.

1 3 5 6 4 2

Contents

Glossary Words

When a word is printed in **bold**, you can look up its meaning in the Glossary on page 31.

What Is Biodiversity?

Biodiversity, or biological diversity, describes the variety of living things in a particular place, in a particular **ecosystem**, or across the entire Earth.

Measuring Biodiversity

The biodiversity of a particular area is measured on three levels:

- **species** diversity, which is the number and variety of species in the area.
- genetic diversity, which is the variety of **genes** each species has. Genes determine the characteristics of different living things. A variety of genes within a species enables it to **adapt** to changes in its environment.
- ecosystem diversity, which is the variety of **habitats** in the area. A diverse ecosystem has many habitats within it.

White-tailed deer are a part of the biodiversity of North American woodlands.

Species Diversity

Some habitats, such as coral reefs, have very high species diversity. Others have low biodiversity. Some habitats have high biodiversity in particular species. Woodlands in Australia have a large number of nectar-feeding bird species but few species of amphibians, such as frogs and toads.

Habitats and Ecosystems

Woodlands are habitats, which are places where animals and plants live. Within a woodland habitat, there are also many types of smaller habitats, sometimes called microhabitats. Some woodland microhabitats are leaf litter, tree trunks, soil, and the woodland **canopy**. Different kinds of **organisms** live in these places. The animals, plants, other living things, nonliving things, and all the ways they affect each other make up a woodland ecosystem.

Biodiversity Under Threat

The variety of species on Earth is under threat. There are somewhere between 5 million and 30 million species on Earth. Most of these species are very small and hard to find, so only about 1.75 million have been described and named. These are called known species.

Scientists estimate that as many as fifty species become **extinct** every day. Extinction is a natural process, but human activities have sped up the rate of extinction by nearly one thousand times.

Known Species of Organisms on Earth

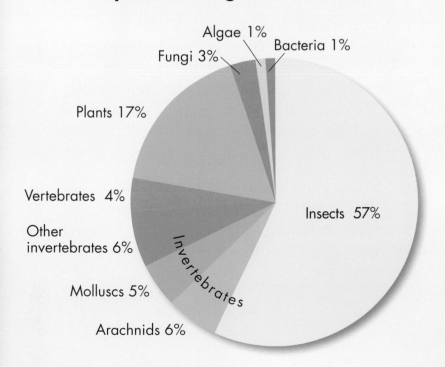

Algae 1%
Bacteria 1%
Fungi 3%
Plants 17%
Vertebrates 4%
Other invertebrates 6%
Molluscs 5%
Arachnids 6%
Invertebrates
Insects 57%

The known species of organisms on Earth can be divided into bacteria, algae, fungi, plant, and animal species. Animal species are further divided into vertebrates and invertebrates.

Approximate Numbers of Known Vertebrate Species

ANIMAL GROUP	KNOWN SPECIES
Fish	31,000
Birds	10,000
Reptiles	8,800
Amphibians	6,500
Mammals	5,500

Why Is Biodiversity Important?

Biodiversity is important for many reasons. The diverse organisms in an ecosystem take part in natural processes essential to the survival of all living things. Biodiversity produces food and medicine. It is also important to people's quality of life.

Natural Processes

Human survival depends on the natural processes that go on in ecosystems. Through natural processes, air and water are cleaned, waste is decomposed, **nutrients** are recycled, and disease is kept under control. Natural processes depend on the organisms that live in the soil, on the plants that produce oxygen and absorb **carbon dioxide**, and on the organisms that break down dead plants and animals. When species of organisms become extinct, natural processes may stop working.

Food

We depend on biodiversity for our food. The world's major food plants are grains, vegetables, and fruits. These plants have all been bred from plants in the wild. Wild plants are important sources of genes for breeding new disease-resistant crops. If these wild plants were to become extinct, their genes would be lost.

Medicine

About 40 percent of all prescription drugs come from chemicals that have been extracted from plants. Scientists discover new, useful plant chemicals every year. The National Cancer Institute discovered that 70 percent of plants found to have anticancer properties were rain forest plants.

When plant species become extinct, the chemicals within them are lost forever. The lost chemicals might have been important in the making of new medicines.

Did You Know?

Rice is one of the most important food crops in the world. Many cultures eat rice, but it is especially popular in Asia, where it was first grown. Its species name is *Oryza sativa*. Humans began **cultivating** rice more than 10,000 years ago.

Quality of Life

Biodiversity is important to our quality of life. Animals and plants inspire wonder and they are part of our **heritage**. Some species have become particularly important to us. If the giant panda became extinct, our survival would not be affected, but we would feel great sadness and regret. The giant panda is a powerful symbol of threatened woodland biodiversity.

Animal species such as the giant panda inspire people's wonder and imagination. This improves their quality of life.

Woodlands of the World

A woodland is like a very open forest, with small to medium trees growing far enough apart that their canopy covers between 20 and 50 percent of the sky. There are woodlands on all continents except Antarctica.

Where Woodlands Are Found

Woodlands usually grow in areas that have too little rainfall to support dense forests but enough rainfall for some trees to grow. Woodlands may cover large areas or be isolated, smaller pockets within a larger area of forest. Woodlands often cover the land found between forests and grasslands, between areas of high rainfall and low rainfall.

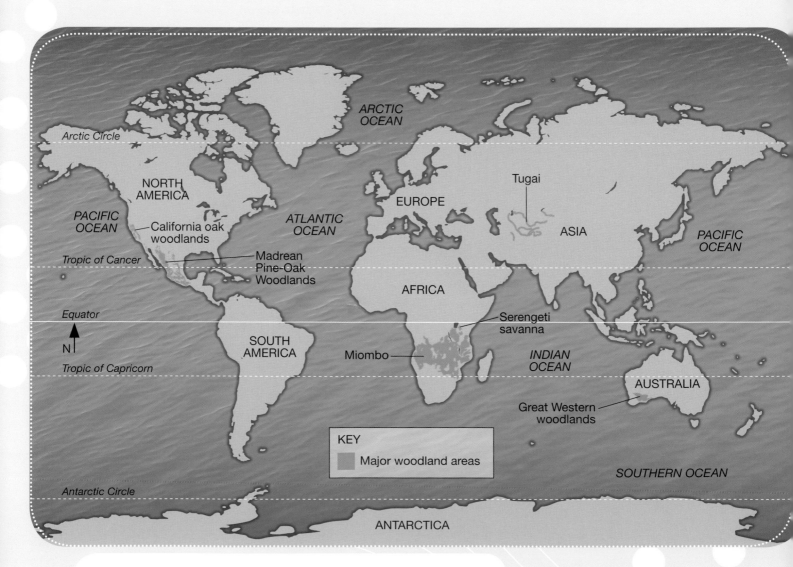

ARCTIC OCEAN

Arctic Circle

NORTH AMERICA

PACIFIC OCEAN

California oak woodlands

Tropic of Cancer

Madrean Pine-Oak Woodlands

ATLANTIC OCEAN

EUROPE

Tugai

ASIA

PACIFIC OCEAN

AFRICA

Equator

N

SOUTH AMERICA

Serengeti savanna

Miombo

INDIAN OCEAN

Tropic of Capricorn

AUSTRALIA

Great Western woodlands

KEY

Major woodland areas

SOUTHERN OCEAN

Antarctic Circle

ANTARCTICA

This map shows the major woodlands mentioned in this book.

Types of Woodlands

Different regions have different types of woodlands. Each woodland type has different plant and animal species.

Tugai Woodlands, Central Asia

Tugai woodlands grow on the plains along several rivers in central Asia. Deserts surround the tugai and the woodlands are extremely important to many animal species, such as about 150 species of **migratory birds**, which rest, feed, and drink in the woodlands on their migrations. Tugai woodlands are highly threatened by human activities, particularly farming.

Miombo Woodlands, Southern Central Africa

Miombo woodlands cover around 1 million square miles (2.7 million square kilometers) of southern central Africa. They are dominated by different species of miombo trees. Grasses grow densely beneath the trees. There is a long dry season when fires burn the dry grass.

Great Western Woodlands, Western Australia

The Great Western woodlands are one of the largest areas of **temperate** woodland in the world, covering 60,000 square miles (160,000 sq km). More than 3,000 plant species are found here, which is 30 percent of Australia's total number of plant species and more than twice the number found in the United Kingdom. Nonnative weeds are a threat to this biodiversity, and **invasive species** such as foxes and cats are a major threat to native mammal species.

Great Western woodland

Open Woodland

Because sunlight can reach most of the ground, a woodland may have many grasses and shrubs growing between the trees. Woodlands that are very open and have trees scattered throughout a grassy landscape are called **savannas**.

Miombo woodland

Woodland Biodiversity

Each type of woodland has its own biodiversity. Soil type determines which species of trees grow in the woodland, and this **vegetation** determines which animal species live there. African savannas, for example, have lots of grasses so there are many species of large mammals.

Soil Types

Soil types vary. They can be well-drained or partly drained, fertile or infertile. Miombo woodlands are found in soils that are quite infertile and the vegetation that grows is of poor nutritional value. Large grazing animals such as elephants consume this vegetation in large quantities and can survive in these woodlands. Giraffes, which need highly nutritious leaves, are rare in miombo woodlands. In the western United States, much of the soil is rocky and only well-adapted types of plants can grow there. Certain types of pine and cypress trees thrive in this soil.

Grazing Mammals

The **tropical** woodlands of Africa are home to many species of grass-eating mammals, such as antelopes. In Australia's tropical woodlands, there are few species of large grazing mammals, and termites consume the most grass of any animal by far.

A tall termite mound sits beside a tree in an Australian woodland.

African Savannas

The Serengeti National Park in Tanzania is rich in biodiversity. It has the world's greatest concentration of large mammals. Throughout the grassland of the park are large areas of savanna, where acacias are the main type of tree. These woodlands are habitat for **herbivores** including warthogs, bushbucks, sitatungas, duikers, impalas, and dik-diks. Leopards prey on these animals, using the trees for cover while hunting. Lions rest in the shade of the trees. Vervet monkeys and olive baboons forage in the savanna and climb into the trees for safety.

Large herbivores such as giraffes feed on the acacia leaves. Elephants also feed on the acacia leaves, often pushing whole trees over to reach them. This grazing behavior helps keep the savanna canopy open. Regular summer fires prevent acacia trees from growing too densely and allow grass to grow between the trees.

Did You Know?

In 1900, there were more than 100,000 black rhinoceroses in Africa. Today there are about 4,000. The cause of this decline is **poaching**. Rhinoceroses are shot and their horns are cut off and sold for traditional Chinese medicines.

Animals gather to drink and bathe at a water hole in the Serengeti savanna in Tanzania.

Woodland Ecosystems

Living and nonliving things, and the **interactions** between them, make up woodland ecosystems. Living things are plants and animals. Nonliving things include the rocks, soil, and water, as well as the **climate**.

Food Chains and Food Webs

A very important way that different species interact is by eating or consuming other species. This transfers energy and nutrients from one organism to another. A food chain illustrates this flow of energy, by showing what eats what. A food web shows how many different food chains fit together.

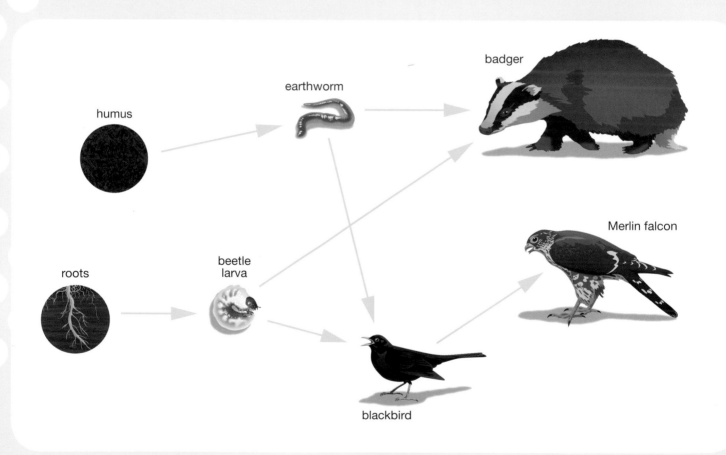

This European woodland food web is made up of several food chains. In one food chain, roots are eaten by beetle larvae, which are eaten by blackbirds, which in turn are eaten by Merlin falcons.

Other Interactions

Nonliving things and living things in a woodland interact in other ways, too. Many owls in the United States nest in tree hollows. These hollows are created when branches break off old trees, allowing fungi to rot away the exposed wood.

Fire and Plant Growth

Fire is an important part of a woodland ecosystem. Fire kills tree seedlings and promotes the growth of grass.

Woodland fires occur naturally or are caused by humans. Over thousands of years, indigenous Australians used fire to keep woodlands open and attract grazing animals for hunting. When European settlers arrived in Australia in 1788, burning-off ended and large areas of woodland became thick forests. This change brought about changes to woodland biodiversity. Grasses could not survive in the reduced light and grazing animals could not survive without the grasses.

Changing Ecosystems

Scientists have found that reduced fire in the woodland ecosystems of northern Australia has affected the survival of endangered golden-shouldered parrot chicks. Reduced fire led to more trees and more perching places for butcherbirds. These **predators** took the parrot chicks when they came to the entrance of their hollows to take food from their parents.

Golden-shouldered parrots perch on a tree stump in an Australian woodland. These parrots are endangered because much of their woodland habitat is turning into forest.

Threats to Woodland Biodiversity

Woodlands are among the world's most threatened ecosystems. The Madrean Pine-Oak woodlands is considered a biodiversity hotspot, but it is under threat due to human activity.

Biodiversity Hotspots

A biodiversity hotspot is an area that has a high number of **endemic species**. It is also an area in which biodiversity is mainly intact, but is under threat from activities such as agricultural and **urban** development, wildlife trade, and pollution.

Madrean Pine-Oak Woodlands

The Madrean Pine-Oak woodlands hotspot covers a large part of the mountainous interior of Mexico and part of the United States. It has rich biodiversity. It is home to more than 5,300 species of flowering plants and 3,925 endemic plant species. The hotspot includes a wide range of woodland ecosystems, from woodlands that are all pine to woodlands that are all oak.

KEY
■ Madrean Pine-Oak woodlands

Arctic Circle

PACIFIC OCEAN

NORTH AMERICA

San Francisco •
Los Angeles •
Ciudad Juarez

Tropic of Cancer

Mexico City •

N

Animal Species of the Madrean Pine-Oak Woodlands

ANIMAL GROUP	NUMBER OF KNOWN SPECIES	NUMBER OF KNOWN ENDEMIC SPECIES
Birds	525	At least 20
Reptiles	At least 380	About 40
Mammals	330	About 6
Amphibians	About 200	About 50
Butterflies	At least 160	45
Freshwater fish	About 80	20

The Madrean Pine-Oak woodlands hotspot is located in Mexico and the southern United States.

Major Threats to the Madrean Pine-Oak Woodlands

In the Madrean Pine-Oak woodlands, just 350 square miles (920 sq km) of the 1,780 square miles (4,620 sq km) of original vegetation remain. Logging has been the main cause of this decline. Some plants are also stolen for sale to gardeners. Fires are a natural part of the woodland ecosystem, but there has been more burning to clear land for cattle grazing. The hotspot is now broken up into smaller areas of forest, which means that many species live in isolated populations. The populations have to breed within their own group and this leads to a fall in genetic diversity.

The Madrean Pine-Oak woodlands habitat is rich in plant biodiversity. It is a hotspot that is under threat.

Firewood Collection and Land Clearing

Firewood collection from woodlands is a major threat to woodland biodiversity and is increasing in many areas. Large areas of woodlands have been logged for lumber and cleared for buildings and roads.

Firewood

Woodland biodiversity is greatly affected by firewood collection. Firewood may be wood that is lying on the woodland floor, dead limbs or dead trees, or even living trees that are cut down to be burned when the wood dries out. Cutting down trees opens up the woodland to invasion by grasses and other weeds. Removal of dead lumber takes away the habitat of many ground-dwelling animals, such as lizards, beetles, and frogs.

Rocks in Woodlands

The woodlands north of Sydney, Australia, are home to the endangered broad-headed snake. It spends the winter in tree hollows, and it basks on rocks and cliffs in the summer. The removal of rocks for gardens is a major threat to the survival of this endangered species.

An area of woodland is logged and cleared to make room for farms, roads, and houses.

Land Clearing

When a patch of woodland is cleared to make way for a road, building, or farm, the biodiversity of the woodland around it is affected. Many species of animals and plants become isolated from one another. One large population of a species may be split into several small populations. In time, these small populations inbreed and lose genetic diversity. The species becomes vulnerable to disease and genetic defects that reduce the species' ability to survive and reproduce.

Roads and houses that are built on the cleared land increase the likelihood of weeds invading woodlands. Unsupervised pet dogs and cats wander from the homes and prey on local woodland species.

Eucalyptus woodland is cleared for development in Tasmania, Australia.

Woodland Clearing in Australia

Australia has lost more woodland than most countries in the past two hundred years. One-third of its eucalyptus woodland has been cleared since European settlers arrived in Australia in 1788. Today, just 8 percent of Australia's remaining woodlands are protected in reserves, such as national parks.

Most of Australia's remaining woodland is unprotected.

Eucalyptus Woodland in Australia

Area remaining in 2005 that was protected in reserves: 27,580 sq mi (71,440 sq km)

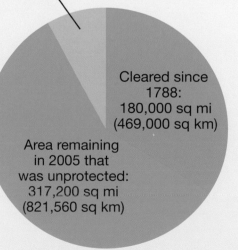

Cleared since 1788: 180,000 sq mi (469,000 sq km)

Area remaining in 2005 that was unprotected: 317,200 sq mi (821,560 sq km)

Nonnative species are introduced both deliberately and accidentally to woodland ecosystems. Some of these become invasive species and threaten the biodiversity of the woodlands.

Introduced and Invasive Species

Introduced species are nonnative species that are brought into a habitat. Some introduced species become invasive species, changing the woodland ecosystem.

The common rhododendron and the gray squirrel are invasive species. The common rhododendron is a colorful flowering shrub native to Europe and Asia. It was brought to the United Kingdom as a garden plant in the late 1700s. Since then, it has become invasive in many British woodlands, crowding out native shrubs as it spreads. Another introduced species in British woodlands is the gray squirrel. This rodent was brought to the United Kingdom from North America in the 1800s. Since then it has spread widely, overwhelming the native red squirrel, which is now endangered in the United Kingdom.

Wombats and Buffel Grass

The last seventy northern hairy-nosed wombats in the world live in a patch of woodland in Queensland, Australia. This habitat has been invaded by buffel grass, a grass species introduced from Africa for grazing. Wombats do not eat buffel grass and the weed crowds out plants that the wombats do eat. The survival of the northern hairy-nosed wombat depends on buffel grass being eradicated, wiped out, or controlled.

Rhododendrons are an invasive species that have spread through woodland habitats in the United Kingdom.

Buffel grass thrives in foreign habitats, overwhelming the native plants that are eaten by local animals.

How Are Species Introduced?

Many invasive species are introduced deliberately. Buffel grass, an African species, was introduced for cattle grazing in countries such as the United States and Australia. It has spread widely through woodlands. Other invasive species are not spread deliberately. They might be introduced in a delivery of goods from another part of the world.

Why Do Some Species Become Invasive?

Introduced species thrive because there are often no diseases that affect them or animals that eat them in their new habitat. Introduced plants are often well adapted to areas affected by human activities such as logging. Logging disturbs the soil, giving weed seeds a place to start growing and crowd out native plants.

RECEIVE IT, TREAT
Wildlife Trade and Hunting

The illegal trade in animals is worth about $160 billion a year. Many species that are traded are caught in woodlands. Some animals are hunted for their meat.

Demand for Wild Animals

There is a huge demand for wild animals. This demand comes mainly from:

- animal collectors
- buyers and sellers of traditional Chinese medicines
- restaurants selling bush meat to customers
- the illegal pet trade.

Rare Animals

Animal collectors pay large amounts of money for all kinds of animals, particularly reptiles, small mammals, and brightly colored birds and their eggs. If an animal is rare, collectors will pay even larger amounts. This money is motivation for people to hunt and capture rare animals. **Poachers** may be very poor people who need money to provide for their families, or they may be people who simply want to grow rich.

Elephant-foot stools and stuffed endangered animals are just some of the wild animal products seized from smugglers.

Smugglers Caught

In May 2008 Russian police arrested six people involved in attempting to smuggle 900 bear paws, 4 Siberian tiger skins and more than 32 pounds (60 kilograms) of tiger bones into China. These items were to be used to make traditional Chinese medicines. The six men were sentenced to jail terms ranging from four to seven years.

Traditional Chinese Medicines

The use of tigers and rhinoceroses in traditional Chinese medicines has been a major cause of the decline in the numbers of these animals. It is illegal to bring these animals and their products into China, but there are still many stores around the world that sell medicines made from these animals. As long as people believe that these medicines are beneficial there is likely to be demand for them.

Bush Meat

Poverty, hunger, and greed are all motives for people to hunt and kill wild animals for food. In Africa's Serengeti National Park, around 40,000 savanna animals are killed each year for their meat and body parts.

International Commitment on Illegal Trade

In July 2008, the leaders of the world's eight richest countries, called the G8, recommitted to increasing efforts to reduce the rate of biodiversity loss. Their goal is to reduce "threats from the **illicit** trade in wildlife."

It is illegal to trade ivory in most countries, but many elephants are still killed for their ivory tusks.

Climate Change

The world's average temperature is rising because levels of certain gases, such as carbon dioxide, are increasing in Earth's atmosphere. This global warming is causing changes to the world's climate. These changes are affecting woodland biodiversity.

Changing Rainfall

Rainfall is an important part of a woodland ecosystem. Usually, woodlands grow where annual rainfall is between 12 and 24 inches (30–60 centimeters), which is too little for dense forests to grow, but enough for some trees to survive. Climate change is changing rainfall patterns in different parts of the world. Where rainfall decreases, woodlands are likely to become more open. Some woodlands may become grasslands and some forests may become woodlands.

Increased Fires

The rising temperatures caused by climate change will likely increase the number of woodland fires and their intensity. Fire kills trees, but grasses regrow soon after being burned. With an increase in the number of fires, grasses will eventually replace trees and shrubs. Animals that feed or shelter in trees and shrubs will lose their habitat. Species that live among the grasses or eat grass seeds may increase in number.

Climate change will increase the likelihood and intensity of woodland fires.

In Australia, climate change may lead to more habitats for feral pigs.

Other Climate Changes

It is hard to tell how much woodland biodiversity will be affected by climate change. Plant and animal species that are currently restricted by climate conditions may spread. For example, an increase in rainfall in northern Australia will enable feral pigs to spread into woodland areas that are currently too dry for them. An increase in temperature of just a few degrees Fahrenheit may enable the cane toad, an invasive species, to spread into woodland and other habitats as far south as Sydney.

Did You Know?

Five thousand years ago, much of the Sahara Desert was fertile woodland. We know this from rock carvings made at the time. These carvings, in Algeria and elsewhere, show rhinoceroses and other savanna animals.

Woodland Conservation

Conservation is the protection, preservation, and wise use of resources. Conserving woodland biodiversity involves protecting it from threats caused by human activities. Research, education, laws, and breeding projects are very important in woodland conservation.

Research

Research is vital to woodland conservation. Research surveys or studies are used to find out about woodland ecosystems. Scientific studies of biodiversity may be surveys of species, observations of interactions between species, or studies of the habitat requirements of species. The ways in which human activities affect woodland biodiversity are also studied. Ways to conserve biodiversity can be found using the information that is collected.

A scientist collects bark for testing and research.

Education

It is very important to educate people about woodland conservation. When people know about a habitat and the animals that live in it, they are more likely to want to care for it. Research findings are often passed on to the public. People may get involved in revegetation projects or ask their local government representatives to take action to protect woodlands.

Laws and Penalties

Research findings are used by governments to make laws to protect woodlands. Laws and regulations may cover:

- littering
- firewood collection
- camping
- disturbances to wildlife
- removal of plants.

Penalties apply to people who break these laws. Penalties may range from a small fine for littering to prison terms for animal poaching.

Endangered Animal Release

Scientists believe the red wolf once roamed throughout the woodlands, marshes, and other habitats of the southeastern United States and along the East Coast. However, due to hunting and habitat loss, the red wolf was extinct in the wild by 1980. The U.S. Fish and Wildlife Service reintroduced the species into North Carolina in 1987. They are surviving in the 2,300-square-mile (6,000 sq km) reintroduction area, but scientists hope the red wolf will continue breeding and will spread into new areas.

Captive Breeding

Many woodland animal species are so endangered that they must be bred in zoos to ensure their survival. This is called captive breeding. Captive animals can be used to educate people about the needs of species that live in woodlands. Some captive breeding programs involve releasing captively bred animals into the wild.

Captive breeding and habitat protection are ways to increase the populations of endangered species, such as the black rhinoceros.

CASE STUDY:
California Oak Woodlands

Oak woodlands cover about 15,400 square miles (40,000 sq km) of California. These woodlands have among the highest number of endemic mammal species of any ecosystem in the United States.

Biodiversity of the California Oak Woodlands

There are five main **communities** of plants in the California oak woodlands. A different species of oak tree dominates in each community. In the north, Oregon oak dominates. In the south, Engelmann oak is the major species. Among the woodlands are areas of savanna, grassland, and areas of tangled shrubs and bushes, called chaparral.

Approximately 2,000 species of native plants are found in the California oak woodlands. There are also more than 70 species of mammals and about 100 species of birds.

Did You Know?

The giant kangaroo rat, Santa Cruz kangaroo rat, Heermann kangaroo rat, Sonoma chipmunk, and salt marsh harvest mouse are endemic to the oak woodlands of California.

The California oak woodlands are located on the West Coast of the United States.

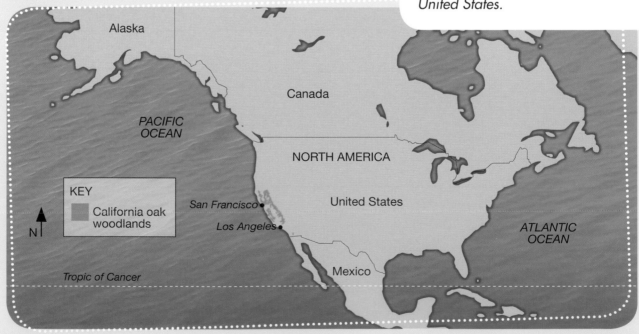

KEY
California oak woodlands

Alaska

Canada

PACIFIC OCEAN

NORTH AMERICA

United States

San Francisco

Los Angeles

ATLANTIC OCEAN

Mexico

Tropic of Cancer

N

Threats to California Oak Woodland Biodiversity

The major threats to the California oak woodlands have been:

- land clearing for vineyards and houses
- cattle and sheep grazing
- firewood collection.

At least 70 percent of the original area of the California oak woodlands has been lost. California's human population is still increasing and putting pressure on the woodlands. The remaining woodlands are under threat, and an estimated 1,160 square miles (3,000 sq km) of woodland is under severe threat.

The introduction of grasses and other weeds has changed woodland ecosystems. Where grasses thrive, fires are fierce and frequent, killing the seedlings of native plants such as oaks.

Climate Change

Scientists have studied how climate change might affect two oak species, the blue oak and valley oak. They concluded that due to changes in temperature and increased rainfall caused by global warming, the areas in which these species can grow will move northward and shrink by half. The ranges of other plant species and the animals that depend on them are likely to change, too.

Blue oak is a tree species that is endemic to the California oak woodlands.

CASE STUDY: California Oak Woodlands

Sudden Oak Death

Sudden Oak Death is a deadly oak disease caused by the fungus *Phytophthora ramorum*, which first appeared in California in the 1990s. The fungus thrives in cool, moist areas along the coast. Plant nurseries also provide ideal conditions due to their watering systems, so the fungus has spread beyond the coast. Because Sudden Oak Death kills particular tree species, including oaks, the fungus changes the biodiversity of areas it invades. With many dead trees, an infected area is likely to have more frequent and fiercer fires.

Controlling Sudden Oak Death

At present, once a tree is infected with the fungus it cannot be saved. The best option may be to slow the spread of *Phytophthora ramorum*. Nurseries close to oak woodlands should ensure that their plants are free of the fungus. Once it is in the wild, preventing the spread of the fungus may be impossible. There, it is spread in soil carried on hikers' boots, vehicle tires, and animals' feet.

Did You Know?

The California Oak Mortality Task Force was formed in 2000. It works to find ways of combating Sudden Oak Death through research, education, and management.

On a hillside in California, trees infected with Sudden Oak Death have died and turned grey.

Protecting the California Oak Woodlands

Protecting the oak woodlands in California is a high priority for the Californian state government, local governments, and community groups.

A member of a Californian oak conservation group works to restore woodland by planting oak seedlings.

Law to Protect the Woodlands

In 2001, the California state government passed the California Oak Woodland Conservation Act. This law recognizes that the California oak woodlands:

- are habitat for many species
- are of great scenic and natural beauty
- prevent **erosion**
- improve water quality
- are important in nutrient recycling through soil and plants
- increase property values.

The law led to the establishment of the Oak Woodland Preservation Program. This program provides money and advice to landowners and community groups to protect and restore oak woodlands in their neighborhoods.

California Oak Woodlands in the Past

The California oak woodlands were described by Charles Nordoff, a traveler, in 1783:

"The country about [the city of] Visalia, for six or eight miles in every direction, looks like an old park, because of its magnificent oaks. These trees, like the oak generally in California, are low-branched, wide-spreading, gnarled; they are magnificent in size; many of them must be hundreds of years old; and they are disposed on the plain in most lovely groups, masses, and single specimens."

What Is the Future of Woodlands?

The future of woodlands depends on how people value them. Attitudes to woodlands are changing and people know that their value is greater than the money that can be made from cutting them down. People are working to protect and restore woodlands.

What Can You Do For Woodlands?

You can help protect woodlands in several ways:

- Find out about woodlands. Why are they important and what threatens them?
- If you live near a woodland, join a volunteer group that replants cleared land with woodland **species**.
- Become a responsible consumer. Do not litter or waste resources, particularly water.
- Choose plants for your garden that will not cause problems for native plants.
- If you are concerned about woodlands in your area, or in other areas, send a letter to or e-mail your local newspaper, your state congressperson, or local representative, and express your concerns. Know what you want to say, set out your argument, be sure of your facts, and ask for a reply.

Useful Websites

💻 **www.worldwildlife.org/wildworld/profiles/terrestrial/na/na1202_full.html**

This website gives information about the biodiversity of the California oak woodlands and conservation activities.

💻 **www.biodiversityhotspots.org**

This website has information about the richest and most threatened areas of biodiversity on Earth.

💻 **www.iucnredlist.org**

The International Union for Conservation of Nature (IUCN) Red List has information about threatened plant and animal species.

Glossary

adapt   Change in order to survive.

canopy   Leaves of the upper layer of plants in a forest or woodland.

carbon dioxide   A colorless and odorless gas produced by plants, animals, and the burning of coal and oil.

climate   The weather conditions in a certain region over a long period of time.

communities   Groups of species living in a particular area.

cultivating   Growing plants as crops.

ecosystem   The living and nonliving things in a certain area and the interactions between them.

endemic species   Species found only in a particular area.

erosion   Wearing away of soil and rock by wind or water.

extinct   Having no living members.

genes   Segments of deoxyribonucleic acid (DNA) in the cells of a living thing, which determine characteristics.

habitats   Places where animals, plants, or other living things live.

herbivores   Plant-eating animals.

heritage   Things we inherit and pass on to future generations.

illicit   Forbidden by law.

interactions   Actions that are taken together or that affect each other.

invasive species   Nonnative species that negatively affect their new habitats.

migratory birds   Birds that fly from one part of the world to another, and back, each year.

nutrients   Substances that are used by living things for growth.

organisms   Animals, plants, and other living things.

poaching   Hunting or taking illegally.

predators   Animals that kill and eat other animals.

savannas   Very open woodlands with grass between the trees.

species   A group of animals, plants, or other living things that share the same characteristics and can breed with one another.

temperate   In a region or climate that has mild temperatures.

tropical   In the hot and humid region between the Tropic of Cancer and the Tropic of Capricorn.

urban   Of towns and cities.

vegetation   Plants.

Index